KT-155-439

The Wild Life of ELK

Written by
Donna Love

Illustrated by
Christina Wald

The Wild Life of Elk

Written by Donna Love
Illustrations by Christina Wald

Library of Congress Cataloging-in-Publication Data

Love, Donna, 1956-
The wild life of elk / written by Donna Love ; illustrated by Christina Wald. — 1st ed.
    p. cm.
Includes index.
ISBN 978-0-87842-579-2 (pbk. : alk. paper)
1. Elk—Juvenile literature. 2. Elk—Habitat—Juvenile literature. I. Wald, Christina, ill. II. Title.
QL737.U55L683 2011
599.65'7--dc22

                    2011014779

© 2011 Rocky Mountain Elk Foundation
5705 Grant Creek Rd · Missoula, MT 59808
800-CALL ELK · www.RMEF.org

Printed in Hong Kong

This book belongs to:

_____

The Rocky Mountain Elk Foundation & U.S. Forest Service Partnership

The Rocky Mountain Elk Foundation and the U.S. Forest Service have worked together as partners since 1984. As partners, they have enhanced or protected over 2.7 million acres of elk habitat on the national forests and grasslands across the United States. During that time, the population of elk in the United States grew from approximately 500,000 to more than 1 million animals.

The mission of the Rocky Mountain Elk Foundation is to ensure the future of elk, other wildlife and their habitat.

WWW.RMEF.ORG

The mission of the USDA Forest Service is to sustain the health, diversity and productivity of the nation's forests and grasslands to meet the needs of present and future generations.

WWW.FS.FED.US/

Recognition

This book was made possible by the exceptional support of the "RMEF/USFS Children's Elk Book Team"

RMEF: Paul Allen, Paul Queneau, Brandee Sperry, Stephanie Strickland and Tom Toman

USFS: Andrea Bedell-Loucks, Sandy Kratville and Gail Tunberg

Special Thanks to:

Confederated Salish & Kootenai Tribes, Salish-Pend d'Oreille Culture Committee

Grant Parker, RMEF

Jennifer Newbold, Office of General Counsel

Jessi Schott, RMEF

South Dakota State Historical Society

Teresa Asleson, USFS

Historical Photo Credits:

Denver Public Library; Western History Collection, Edward H. Boos, Call #BS-103

Denver Public Library; Western History Collection, Edward H. Boos, Call #BS-117

CONTENTS

What's that animal and what's growing on its head? It's an elk!

Its antlers are growing on its head. Female, or cow elk do not grow antlers—so this elk is a male, or bull elk. In battle, the bull elk uses its antlers as both sword and shield, brandishing them in a fight.

This bull's antlers are massive. They can grow 5-feet long and weigh nearly 70 pounds. Could you carry 70 pounds on your head? An elk can! It is very strong. Count the points on the elk's antlers? Did you count eight points on each side? That means this bull is a monarch, or the largest elk, the *king of the forest*.

The "Antlered Deer"
Elk Around the World

An elk is in the deer family, *Cervidae* (SIR-vuh-dee) which are animals with antlers. Other cervids in North America include moose, caribou, mule deer and white-tailed deer.

White-tailed Deer | Mule Deer | Caribou | Elk | Moose

TINE TIPS

An elk's genus and species name is *Cervus elaphus*. *Cervus* is Latin for antler, and *elaphus* is Latin for deer. So an elk's scientific name means "antler deer."

Elk live in many places around the world. The animal we call elk here in America, we also call wapiti (WAH-pah-tee), a Native American Shawnee tribal name meaning "white rump." Europeans, however, use elk as the name for their moose, while calling their elk "red deer." In Asia, elk-like animals live in many places and go by many common names.

European red deer, Asian elk and North American elk can have babies together and their babies can have babies, which shows that elk from all around the world have close family ties.

Wapiti

European Red Deer

Asian (Manchurian) Elk

Elk live in a group called a herd. How many elk can you count in this herd?

Historically, it is thought that up to 10 million elk roamed North America. In the United States, elk lived just about everywhere except Maine, Connecticut, New Hampshire, Florida and Hawaii. Today, elk live in so many places in the U.S. that they have acquired a variety of regional names. However, all elk are the same species or kind of animal. They just live in different places.

On the Northern Great Plains an elk is called a Manitoban (man-uh-TOE-bahn) elk.

In the Rocky Mountain West an elk is called a Rocky Mountain elk.

On the Pacific Coast an elk is called a Roosevelt's elk.

In the Central Valley of California an elk is called a Tule (TOO-lee) elk

Elk Fossils

The Stag Moose was a large moose-like deer that had an elk-like head and antlers. It lived in North America from Canada to Arkansas during the Pleistocene or most recent Ice Age, and went extinct about 11,500 years ago.

The oldest elk fossils show that elk-like animals have been on Earth for 5.2 million years. The best-preserved and most abundant elk fossils are antlers, but archaeologists have also found skulls, bones and teeth. In Siberia, 200,000-year-old fossils have been found that closely resemble today's elk.

SAKU TAKAKUSAKI

TINE TIPS

Can you name other critters that crossed the Bering land bridge?

Around 40,000 years ago, the earth was covered in glaciers and a land bridge stretched between Asia and North America. The bridge allowed elk to travel between the two continents. Then the earth warmed and the ice melted, flooding the land bridge. Later, the earth froze up again and the spreading ice pushed elk southward where they found prairies and open forests perfect for survival. When the ice melted again, elk had spread across the North American continent from Alaska to Texas and from California to New York.

Home on the Range

Elk Habitat

Today, wild elk roam 28 states in the United States and five Canadian provinces.

Thanks to the devotion of many people, elk have returned to many areas east of the Mississippi River. People who like to hunt elk provide funding and support to improve elk habitat. The most important requirement for elk survival is habitat. Elk love park-like open land, so prairies and grasslands provide a perfect home for some elk, while others live in mountains and forests.

Current U.S. Elk Population: more than 1 million

Kentucky

California beaches

the Tetons

Backyards

Are there wild elk where you live?

Alabama
• Alaska
• Arizona
• Arkansas
• California
• Colorado
Connecticut
Delaware
Florida
Georgia
Hawaii
• Idaho
Illinois
Indiana
Iowa
• Kansas
• Kentucky
Louisiana
Maine
Maryland
Massachusetts
• Michigan
• Minnesota
Mississippi
• Missouri
• Montana
• Nebraska
• Nevada
New Hampshire
New Jersey
• New Mexico
New York
• North Carolina
• North Dakota
Ohio
• Oklahoma
• Oregon
• Pennsylvania
Rhode Island
South Carolina
• South Dakota
• Tennessee
• Texas
• Utah
Vermont
• Virginia
• Washington
West Virginia
• Wisconsin
• Wyoming

• As of 2011

Elk can live in many places—sometimes even right on the edge of town. But no matter where elk live, they need healthy habitat to survive. An elk needs good food to eat, shelter from both scorching heat and frigid cold, fresh, clean water to drink, and plenty of space to roam.

Forested Habitat

The Fitting Room
Elk, Inside & Out

An elk is a tall animal. When the Blackfeet first saw horses they compared the horse to an elk, calling the horse an "elk-dog," meaning that a horse was as tall as an elk, but could be trained to help people like a dog can be.

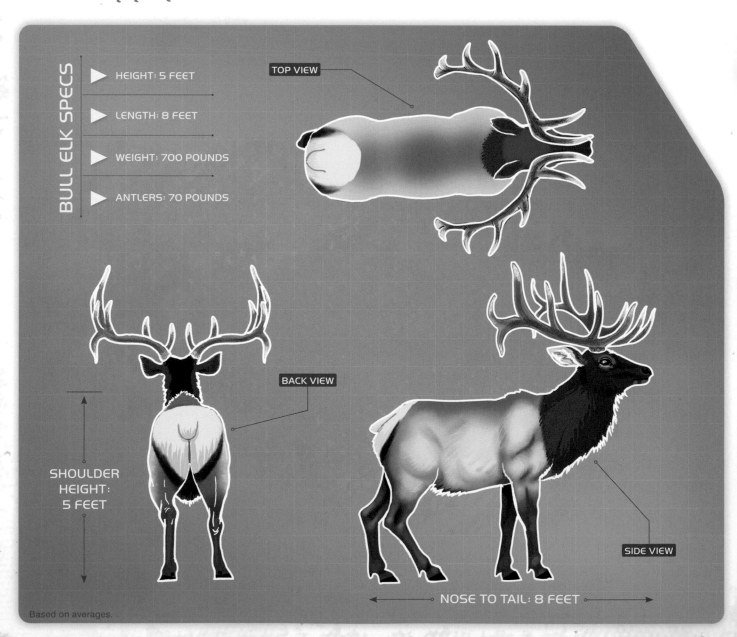

BULL ELK SPECS

▶ HEIGHT: 5 FEET

▶ LENGTH: 8 FEET

▶ WEIGHT: 700 POUNDS

▶ ANTLERS: 70 POUNDS

TOP VIEW

BACK VIEW

SIDE VIEW

SHOULDER HEIGHT: 5 FEET

NOSE TO TAIL: 8 FEET

Based on averages.

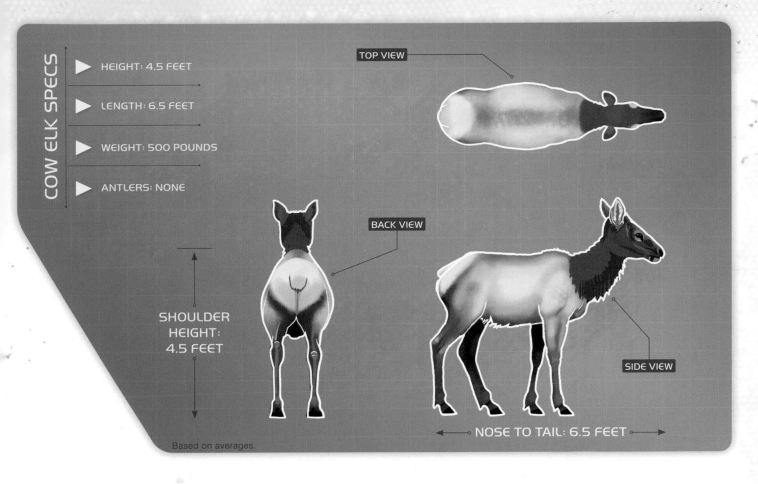

COW ELK SPECS

- ▶ HEIGHT: 4.5 FEET
- ▶ LENGTH: 6.5 FEET
- ▶ WEIGHT: 500 POUNDS
- ▶ ANTLERS: NONE

TOP VIEW

BACK VIEW

SIDE VIEW

SHOULDER HEIGHT: 4.5 FEET

NOSE TO TAIL: 6.5 FEET

Based on averages.

READY. SET. GO!

Even with heavy antlers, an elk can still move!

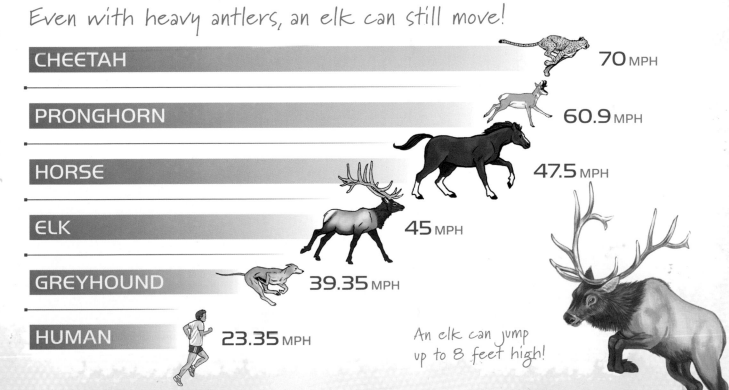

CHEETAH	70 MPH
PRONGHORN	60.9 MPH
HORSE	47.5 MPH
ELK	45 MPH
GREYHOUND	39.35 MPH
HUMAN	23.35 MPH

Based on record bursts of speed, not sustained speed.

An elk can jump up to 8 feet high!

Nature's Camouflage
An Elk's Color

A bull and cow elk are similar in color, though bulls in their winter coats are often lighter.

An elk's color is a perfect camouflage to hide it from predators, which depending on where they live may include mountain lions, wolves, black bears and grizzly bears. While grazing, an elk's darker head and legs look like shadows in the grass. Its lighter back blends in with the distant background.

An elk's mane is dark brown. On its rump, an elk wears a light-colored rump patch, or circle of white, tan or light orange outlined by a dark border. An elk's tail is the same color as its rump patch.

Elk from the Southwest are lighter in color. This helps them blend in with their bright, sunny habitat. Elk that live in Canada and the northern United States, on the other hand, often have brown bodies with dark brown heads, bellies and legs. The dark color of the northern elk is perfect for blending in with shadowy forest habitat.

TINE TIPS

In summer an elk's sleek summer coat is a shiny copper color. In winter an elk's shaggy winter coat is a duller grayish brown.

While lying down, with legs tucked beneath it, an elk looks like the trunk of a dead tree lying on the ground—its ears and head blend with the tree's branches and roots.

Winter Coats & Summer Jackets

An Elk's Hair

In winter, an elk grows hollow guard hairs over its thick undercoat, keeping it dry and warm like a raincoat over a cozy down coat.

Ever notice how some puffy things are warm? That's because they are filled with air. An elk's guard hairs are hollow to provide lofty insulation that traps body heat and keeps the cold out.

In spring, an elk sheds its winter coat and grows a lightweight jacket of short, sleek summer hair. Its hair falls off in thick chunks, leaving the animal looking shaggy and unkempt as its summer coat grows. In autumn, as it sheds its summer hair to make way for its winter coat, an elk looks much more dignified.

Climate Control
The Perfect Temperature for Elk

Do you like to play outside on a warm, sunny day?

An elk's thick skin and hair is perfect for being outside, so it can stand temperatures much colder than you can. Elk love temperatures between 40 and 60 degrees Fahrenheit (5 to 15 Celsius). However, in winter an elk can still be fairly comfortable down to minus 4 degrees Fahrenheit (minus 20 degrees Celsius). But if the temperature stays lower than that for many days, an elk may become cold and weak.

If it's windy and snowy, where would you go to get warm? Would you go inside?

An elk can't go inside, but it does have ways to warm up. On a cold, windy day, an elk seeks protection from blowing wind and snow in low-lying folds in the land, or it beds down in thick and insulating stands of trees. Sometimes elk even huddle together. When an elk lies down, it tucks its legs beneath its body to protect them from the cold.

On the opposite end of the thermometer, an elk is fairly comfortable in its summer coat up to 86 degrees Fahrenheit (30 degrees Celsius). If the temperature gets hotter than that for several days, an elk can become heat-stressed, or too hot. Then it seeks out water and finds shade on north-facing slopes and under trees.

Mud Wallows
Coat Care

Do you like to go swimming on a hot summer day? An elk does, too. An elk can make its own swimming hole by rolling and stomping around on the ground in a wet or damp area in the forest or prairie, creating a mud wallow, or muddy place to roll in. This "wallowing" is practiced mostly by bulls, but cows and calves also enjoy the cooling effect of a mud wallow. Rolling and frolicking in mud, the elk covers its body, which may help ward off insects and may cool the elk during excessive summer heat. Elk also use wallows in fall during mating season. Bulls often urinate in the mud to cover themselves in their scent, and a particular wallow may advertise the presence of a dominant bull that lives in the area to warn other bulls away.

Mud wallows are stinky. Rolling in them in autumn is a perfect way for a bull elk to cover itself with its very own cologne.

Inside Out
An Elk's Skeleton

Can you feel the bones in your fingers and hand? An elk's bones, called its skeleton, help it in the same ways that your skeleton helps you. An elk's skeleton protects its internal organs, supports its weight and helps it move.

Rib Cage
Deep, wide ribs attach to its backbone and curve downward to form a rib cage that protects and supports the elk's large heart and lungs.

Spine
An elk's backbone is sturdy, with a hump above the shoulder. Its spine ends in a short tail.

Legs
An elk's long legs are built for walking on uneven ground, capable of impressive bursts of speed over many miles to escape danger. On flat ground, an elk can run up to 45 miles per hour. On mountains and hillsides, an elk's strong hip and shoulder muscles help it quickly bound uphill or down.

Hock
The hock is a short bone on the back of an elk's ankle that points up and backward. Ligaments attach the hock to the elk's leg for extra strength and stability, allowing the elk to bound up steep hills or run in swift, elegant strides.

ACTIVITY
Feel the back of your ankle. Can you feel the small hollow spot that sits behind and above your heel? That is similar to the way the elk's lower leg is attached to its ankle, leaving a small hollow spot above its ankle between its hock and calf bone.

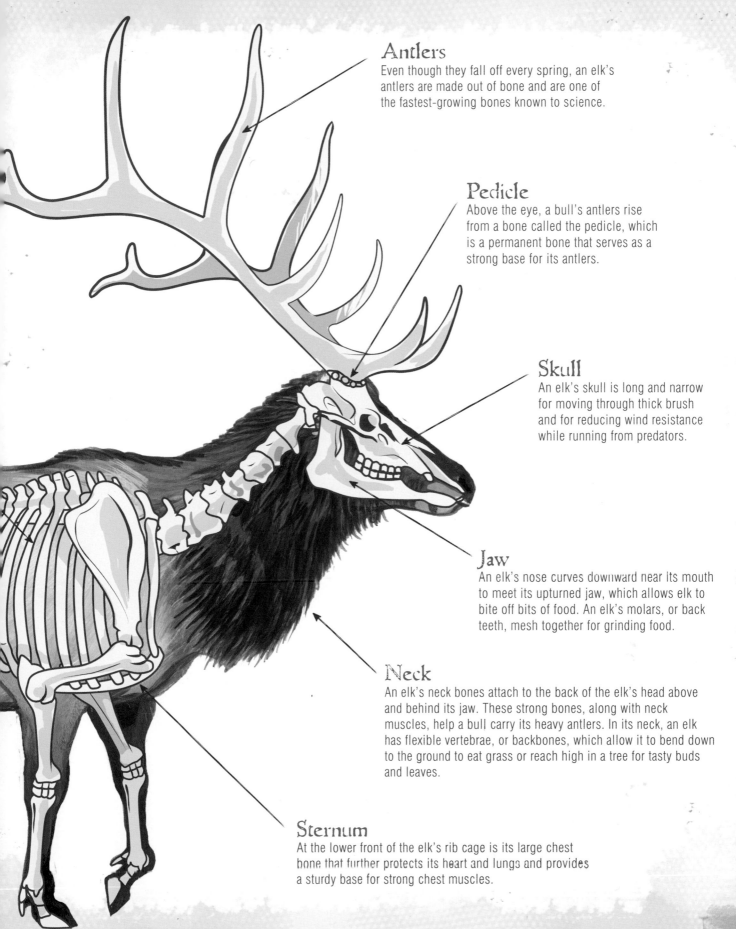

Antlers

Even though they fall off every spring, an elk's antlers are made out of bone and are one of the fastest-growing bones known to science.

Pedicle

Above the eye, a bull's antlers rise from a bone called the pedicle, which is a permanent bone that serves as a strong base for its antlers.

Skull

An elk's skull is long and narrow for moving through thick brush and for reducing wind resistance while running from predators.

Jaw

An elk's nose curves downward near its mouth to meet its upturned jaw, which allows elk to bite off bits of food. An elk's molars, or back teeth, mesh together for grinding food.

Neck

An elk's neck bones attach to the back of the elk's head above and behind its jaw. These strong bones, along with neck muscles, help a bull carry its heavy antlers. In its neck, an elk has flexible vertebrae, or backbones, which allow it to bend down to the ground to eat grass or reach high in a tree for tasty buds and leaves.

Sternum

At the lower front of the elk's rib cage is its large chest bone that further protects its heart and lungs and provides a sturdy base for strong chest muscles.

Making Tracks
An Elk's Hooves

Can you walk on your tiptoes?

An elk always walks on its tiptoes. Elk have four toes on each foot. Two small toes, called dewclaws, are located at the back of its leg. The dewclaws provide balance and extra grip when the elk runs on uneven ground.

Two large, middle toes make up the elk's hoof. These two sturdy toes carry the elk's weight. An elk's hoof has a tight structure, so the two toes don't spread out too wide. This allows an elk to stay up on its tiptoes and run fast.

Elk Sense
Smell, Sound, Sight, Touch

Elk have incredibly keen senses, and they rely on all of them every day to stay alive.

Have you ever tried to sneak close to elk and suddenly felt the wind on your back? About one second later, those elk were probably thundering away. That's because they caught your scent—and elk always trust their noses.

An elk's large ears are situated behind its eyes. They can swivel front to back like a satellite dish, so it can hear sounds coming from every direction. This sharp hearing helps elk stay in contact with each other even in heavy timber or a pitch-black night. They can hear another bull elk's bugle miles away—or a stealthy mountain lion creeping through the grass.

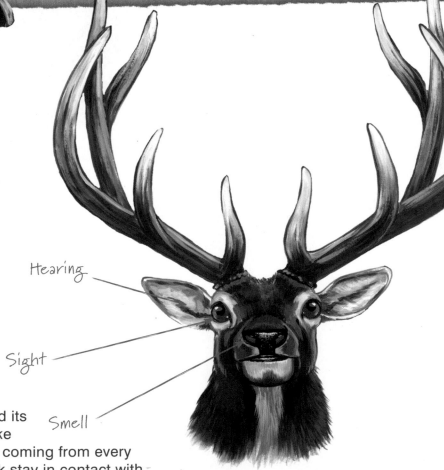

Hearing

Sight

Smell

Now you see me

Sight is also important to elk. An old saying goes, "Eyes on the side, hide. Eyes in front, hunt." So which do you think an elk does? An elk has eyes on the side of its head. It hides from predators. An elk can see in every direction except directly behind or directly in front.

Color me bland

By studying an elk's eye, scientists know that elk can see color. But an elk doesn't see color as brightly as we do, and it can't see or distinguish as many colors as we can. However, an elk's eyesight is designed to detect even the slightest movement, which helps it see when a predator is trying to sneak up on it.

A sense of touch

An elk's sense of touch is similar to ours. When an elk walks through tall grass, it feels the grass sweeping its legs. If an elk's back feels itchy, it might scratch against a tree branch.

What an elk sees

What a person sees

Prime Time Bulls

If you grew antlers, what would you use them for?
An elk uses its antlers as a tool to scratch its back, dig
mud wallows and scrape trees to mark its territory.

But the main reason an elk has antlers is to show its importance to other elk. A bull with large antlers is often the healthiest, so a cow elk considers a bull's antlers to decide which bull to mate with. A healthy bull is also strong, so it often becomes the dominant, or toughest male, and other bulls won't fight it.

Pedicle

FEBRUARY 15 ———➤ MARCH 1 ———➤ MAY 1 ——

As antlers grow they slowly lengthen, expand and branch out. If an antler is broken or injured while growing, it might continue to grow, but it could be smaller than the other antler or misshapen. A set of misshapen antlers, or antlers that are not "mirror images" of each other, are called nontypical antlers. Each year a bull's antlers grow for a longer period of time. A 1-year-old elk, or yearling, grows antlers for about 90 days in its second summer of life. These small antlers are called spikes.

TINE TIPS

The bond between the antler and the pedicle is so strong that 10 bowling balls could hang from each side and the antler wouldn't break off.

A bull's antlers are made from rapidly growing bone. In fact, antlers are the fastest growing bone in the world. Antlers fall off and regrow every year. In late winter or early spring, within about 30 days of losing the previous year's antlers, new antlers begin to grow.

While an antler is growing, it is covered in velvet, which is a skin-like substance filled with blood that carries calcium and other minerals to the antler. Velvet is soft and fuzzy, so while the bull is growing antlers, it is "in velvet." While in velvet, an elk's antlers are flexible and very sensitive. An elk is very careful not to hit them on tree trunks or bump them on tree branches, because it will hurt and could deform its antlers.

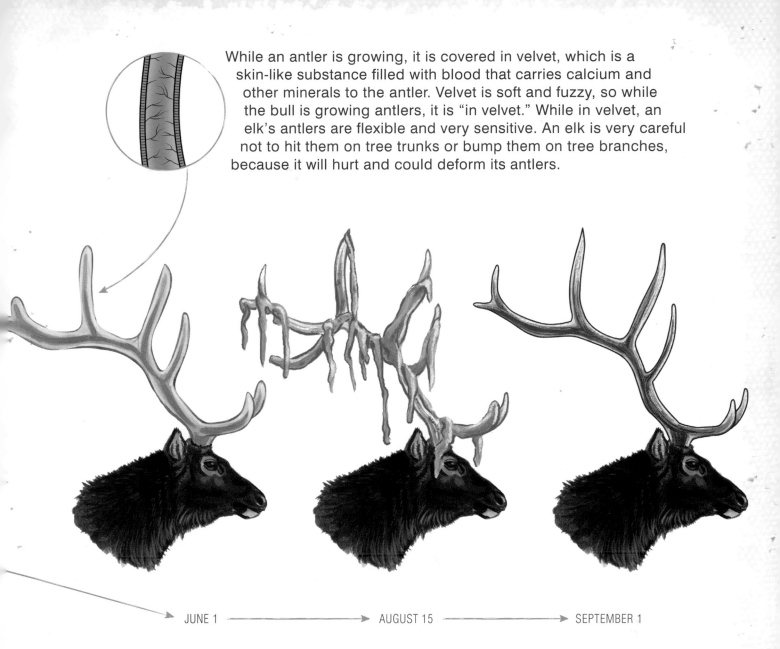

JUNE 1 → AUGUST 15 → SEPTEMBER 1

Two-year-olds grow antlers for about 115 days. 3- and 4-year-old bulls grow antlers for about 140 days. Prime bulls, 5 to 10 years of age, grow antlers for 140-150 days, which is when antlers obtain their largest size.

For the first 60 days, antler growth is slow. After the summer solstice, when summer days begin to shorten again, growth speeds up. How big a bull's antlers get depends in part on its age and whether its father and grandfather had large antlers. However, nutrition is the single most important factor influencing antler size. An elk in healthy habitat with lots of nutritious food to eat grows the largest antlers.

Stripped Away
Velvet and Rub Trees

When antlers are done growing, they begin to mineralize, or harden, and blood inside the velvet stops flowing.

This appears to make velvet very itchy, because after months of careful upkeep, bulls suddenly start tearing it off in long strips by rubbing their antlers against anything they can find.

Soon the velvet strips hang like a mop from a bull's antlers, and in only a few hours dry and fall off, leaving antlers clean and bone-white. Yet bulls keep rubbing their antlers on trees and brush after the velvet is gone, which, through a chemical reaction, darkens them to a deep brown or almost black, depending on the vegetation. Finally, the strong and glorious antlers are complete, and the bull wears them for the next six months.

If you are hiking in a forest and see bark that has been brushed or pulled off a tree trunk, you may be looking at a 'rub tree'.

Look for hair caught in the sap or along the edges of the bark still on the tree. If you find elk hair or the mark is more than 4 feet off the ground, you know an elk was probably rubbing its antlers there!

Cast Off
Antler Sheds

Bull elk usually shed or cast off their antlers between January and March. Antlers found on the ground are sometimes called "sheds" or "casts." It doesn't hurt the elk to lose its antlers. One day one antler falls off, and usually within a few days the other falls off. A bull elk can live to be more than 15 years old. As the bull nears 10 years old, its antlers begin to get smaller. Then a younger bull reaching its prime will take its place as the strongest bull in the herd.

TINE TIPS

Searching for sheds is a great way to get out on a spring treasure hunt! Check local rules, though, before you venture out.

Brow Tine
Antler Parts

Royal Tine
The **sixth tine** is called the royal. It sits on the beam where it bends backward. Many bulls never grow more than six tines.

Beam
The **main branch** of the antler is called the beam. The beam can grow up to 7 inches around. The beams are long and can spread 4 feet wide.

Front View

Burr
The **base** of the antler is called the burr. On an adult bull the burr can be up to 9 inches around.

Typical Bull

WILDVISIONS.NET

Nontypical Bull

PAUL QUENEAU

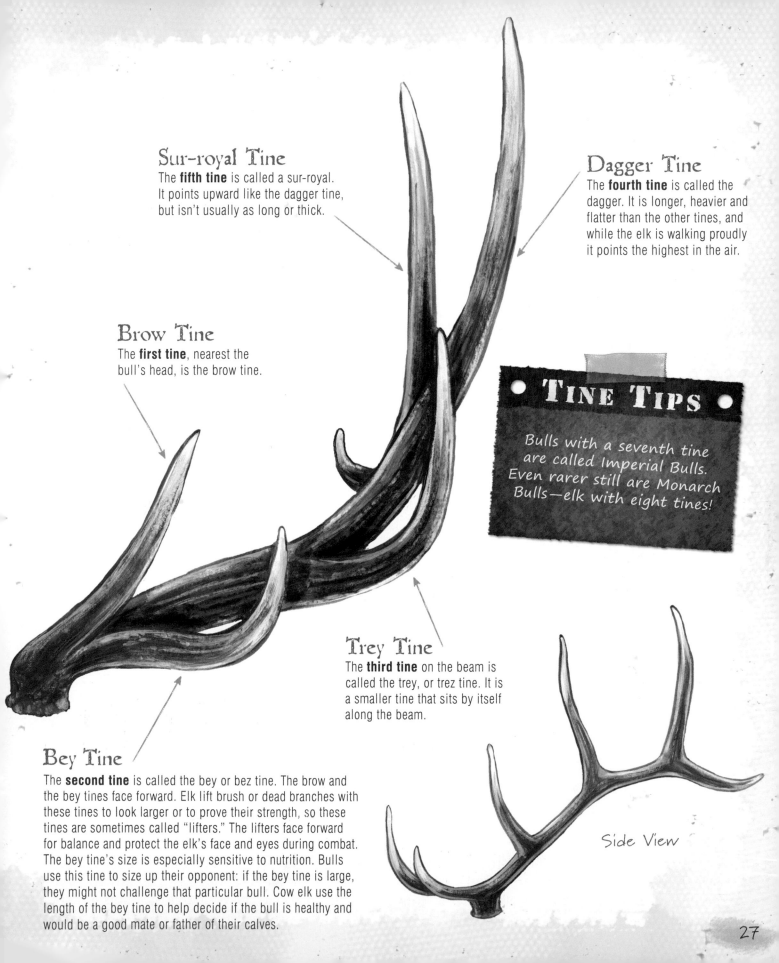

Sur-royal Tine

The **fifth tine** is called a sur-royal. It points upward like the dagger tine, but isn't usually as long or thick.

Dagger Tine

The **fourth tine** is called the dagger. It is longer, heavier and flatter than the other tines, and while the elk is walking proudly it points the highest in the air.

Brow Tine

The **first tine**, nearest the bull's head, is the brow tine.

TINE TIPS

Bulls with a seventh tine are called Imperial Bulls. Even rarer still are Monarch Bulls—elk with eight tines!

Trey Tine

The **third tine** on the beam is called the trey, or trez tine. It is a smaller tine that sits by itself along the beam.

Side View

Bey Tine

The **second tine** is called the bey or bez tine. The brow and the bey tines face forward. Elk lift brush or dead branches with these tines to look larger or to prove their strength, so these tines are sometimes called "lifters." The lifters face forward for balance and protect the elk's face and eyes during combat. The bey tine's size is especially sensitive to nutrition. Bulls use this tine to size up their opponent: if the bey tine is large, they might not challenge that particular bull. Cow elk use the length of the bey tine to help decide if the bull is healthy and would be a good mate or father of their calves.

Dining Out
What an Elk Eats

An elk is an herbivore, which is an animal that only eats plants. Just like you, an elk needs a nutritious diet to stay healthy.

An elk needs vitamins, protein, carbohydrates and minerals like calcium, iron and salt. Protein is essential for elk to build muscle and grow large antlers. Elk get these nutrients by eating a variety of plants. They will even chew on bones or shed antlers for extra calcium.

In spring and summer, an elk is mostly a grazer, eating grasses, forbs, (low, leafy plants) and sedges (plants near water). All of these are high in nutrition for cows nursing their young and for young elk maturing into yearlings. But grass is low in minerals, so elk also visit forests to browse on mineral-rich shrubs as well as the bark, branches and twigs of trees. They also will lick mineral-rich soil.

In fall and winter, many plants are covered in snow. So although an elk still prefers grasses, it will switch to shrubs, tree bark and needles if grass is buried under deep snow. Shrubs can provide high-quality forage when the elk needs energy to stay warm and to deliver healthy babies in spring.

Eat and Run
An Elk's 4x4 Stomach

What if every time you ate, you had to watch for predators that might sneak up and eat you?

Would you eat as much as you could as fast as you could, then find a place to hide while you digest your food? That's what an elk does.

TINE TIPS

Chewing up plants wears down an elk's teeth. This leaves rings on their teeth that biologists can use to estimate their age—just like tree rings!

An elk quickly bites off bits of food with its front teeth and then pushes the food to the back of its mouth with its tongue, grinds it slightly and swallows. An elk has lots of saliva to help rough, lightly chewed food slide easily down its throat. Then it grabs another mouthful of food and quickly swallows again to get as much food as it can into its stomach until it can take cover.

Once it feels safe, an elk spits up its food to chomp on it even more!

Turn the page to see how this works.

Rumen

The first chamber in an elk's stomach is the rumen, which, like a large storage tank, holds lots of food. This allows the elk to eat as much as it can in as little time as possible. Then the elk finds a safe place to watch for danger while it completes digestion.

Reticulum

While it rests, an elk regurgitates, or throws up, food from the rumen and chews it into smaller pieces. The food is then re-swallowed into a second chamber of the stomach, called the reticulum, where it is sorted by size. Pieces that are still too large to be digested are again regurgitated and re-chewed by the elk.

Abomasum

Finally, the food enters the abomasum, which is the last chamber in an elk's stomach. The abomasum is the "true stomach" where the food is broken down into very tiny pieces before entering the small intestine, where nutrients in the food are absorbed into the elk's body.

Omasum

Food re-chewed into small pieces is passed on to the next chamber, the omasum, where moisture is removed.

The food an elk regurgitates is called cud. The elk grinds cud with its back teeth, working its jaw back and forth. This looks pretty silly, but at least the elk chews the cud with its mouth closed!

The tougher the plant, the longer it takes to digest. Tender lupine leaves take 8 hours. Tough huckleberry stems take up to 20 hours. What the elk doesn't use is expelled from its body in the form of half-inch-long, oblong pellets it poops onto the ground. These pellets are similar to those of a deer, but larger and shaped like fat little footballs.

BULL ELK   COW ELK

Actual Size!

Nighty-Night
How an Elk Sleeps

Do you sleep soundly, or do you wake up at every noise?

An elk takes small naps throughout the day, but it doesn't sleep soundly because it is always listening for danger nearby. When it sleeps, an elk lies down on its stomach with its legs tucked underneath. A calf, or baby elk, may lie down on its side, but a fully grown elk rarely does. If a predator sneaks up, an elk will jump up and run, sometimes for great distances, to seek out another safe hideout.

Elk feed day or night.

An elk feeds for as long as necessary to fill its stomach. Then it moves to a secluded spot to lie down and chew its cud. After chewing, it naps. An elk will repeat the daily cycle of eating, chewing cud and sleeping throughout the morning, afternoon and evening.

In healthy habitat an elk needs to feed for up to 9 hours a day, eating 18 pounds of food. In cold weather, a cow providing milk to a calf may need to feed longer to take in all the nutrients it needs.

In spring and summer, grass is perfect for elk cows and calves. Bulls don't help raise calves, so during spring and summer, a bull will leave the herd to seek out protein-rich forbs and shrubs for growing its antlers.

A Family Affair
The Culture of Herds

How large is your family?

Do your aunts and uncles and cousins and grandparents live with you?

An elk herd is much like an extended family.

For most of the year, cow elk and their young hang out together. Lead cows direct the herd. Lead cows are strong and dominant with many herd connections and knowledge of the landscape that other cows follow. Bulls re-join the herd in fall for the rut, or breeding season.

Living in a herd is safer than living alone. In a herd many eyes can watch for danger and warn others. If a predator sneaks up, the safest place to be is in the center of the herd. If attacked, the herd runs in many directions at one time, making it difficult for the predator to focus on any one animal. So the larger the herd, the lower the chances of being caught.

REGGIE FLETCHER

The size of the herd depends on the health of the elk habitat and how much space is available.

If the habitat is healthy and there is abundant space to roam, the herd may be large. In smaller areas of healthy habitat, there may be more herds, but fewer elk in each herd. In summer, up to 400 cows may feed and rest together. Herds of over 1,000 can gather on winter range. Because elk are social and live in herds, they have many ways to communicate with each other.

Song and Dance
Elk Talk

One way elk herds communicate with each other is by "talking" using a variety of calls such as soft chirps, bark-like warnings, whistles and whimpering mews. These might mean "Mom! Where are you?" or "Look, something is moving over there!"

Another way elk communicate with each other is with their posture. Most of these postures are subtle or slight. But if an elk needs to, it will leave no doubt about what it's thinking.

RELAXED

HISS-S-S-S-S

ANGRIER

ANGRY

If an elk becomes angry, it lays its ears back, shows its teeth and hisses.

If its nostrils flare and its head is held high, the elk is getting even more upset. If it stamps its foot, the elk is upset enough that it might strike out with its front hooves.

If an elk senses something strange nearby, it may not run away immediately. It may stand alert and keep a close eye on the disturbance.

RESIGNED

ALERT

Elk would rather keep the peace than fight. An elk that decides to back off lowers its head and neck, stretches out its nose and crouches down by lowering its body. This posture says, "I'm sorry, I didn't mean to bother you."

FLEEING

A bull elk in full flight holds its head up and antlers back.

If a herd chooses to run it will follow the lead cow.

35

Knuckle Cracking
Elk Morse Code

Elk live in both grasslands and forests. In grasslands or other open areas, an elk uses eyes, ears and nose to spot danger from a distance. In forested or brushy areas that are more secluded, an elk still uses its senses but also stealth and silence to avoid being detected by a predator.

Elk also have a secret language that most people don't know about.

RANDI MYSSE RISTAU

In thick brush elk can't always see each other, so they don't know who's nearby. To solve this, they listen for the special and unmistakable "click" that comes from the joint of another elk's front leg as it takes a step forward. This click is distinct to each elk. Elk can walk uphill or down, on gravel or grass, in dry or wet areas, but the click remains constant.

Since no elk predators make such a sound, an elk can identify its friends without seeing them. If the clicking stops, it means that the other elk have stopped moving and are aware of an intruder. When danger has passed, some elk begin moving and the clicking resumes.

TINE TIPS

Walking quietly and wearing camouflage can help a predator sneak up on an elk. But if it smells danger, the elk will run. Predators hunt with the wind in their face to blow their scent away from their prey.

ACTIVITY

Blindfold yourself, friends or classmates, and have everyone snap their fingers. Can you tell your friends by their "clicks"? Have everyone move around. Can you tell where they have moved and how far away?

CLICK

Bugle Boy
Elk Romance

In autumn, bull elk move down to lower elevations and seek out cow elk.

Called "the rut," this mating season occurs in early autumn, late enough that last year's calves are no longer nursing, but early enough that once the rut is over there is still time for the elk to feed and rest before the stress of winter sets in.

Want to hear the many sounds elk can make and see big bulls bugling?

Visit www.rmef.org/videos

When the rut begins, a bull will bugle to attract cow elk and challenge other bulls. A bugle begins low, and rises in pitch until it reaches a high, clear bugle-like scream that can be heard for miles. Then the pitch drops and ends with a series of loud grunts that can only be heard for a short distance.

During the rut, a bull moves among a herd and claims as many cows as it can for its harem, which is the group of cows it will breed with. At this time a cow elk chooses which bull it wants to be with. A typical harem is 15 to 30 cows.

While collecting its harem, a bull allows a calf to stay with its mother but drives away other bulls with its antlers.

TINE TIPS

Each bull has a unique bugle. Some are clear and some are scratchy and hoarse.

Fight for the Right
Bull Battles

Do you like to wrestle with a friend for fun?
Do you push and pull and spin your friend around?

Between the time they shed their velvet to when they drop their antlers, bulls spar with each other for practice. They engage antlers, twist their necks, and push and evade their opponent. This sparring is usually harmless and helps establish rank among bulls. Later, during the rut, the sparring turns to fighting and can be violent.

Bulls of unequal strength rarely fight.
But if a bull challenges another bull,
they may
THRASH the GROUND
with their ANTLERS,

Or MARCH
SIDE by SIDE
with each other.

Or **BLUFF CHARGE** their opponent.

If one of the bulls looks away, the fight is usually off.

SHOWING OFF helps bulls gauge each other's fitness, which helps them **AVOID** a **LOSING BATTLE.**

When two **PRIME BULLS FIGHT,** it is a **MIGHTY TEST** of **STRENGTH.**

Antlers often are used as weapons. In a fight, bulls lock antlers with each other, sometimes colliding violently, and crouch low with their legs spread wide. Then they push and twist each other with their antlers, trying to get the other bull off-balance. At the end of the rut, prime bulls sometimes have up to 100 battle scars, but antler wounds rarely result in serious injury or death. When one bull is pushed to the ground or runs away, the other bull has won.

The **WINNING BULL GETS** to **CLAIM** the **HAREM,** which might be just a couple cows or more than 100, depending on how many battles the bull has won.

You're It
Elk Courtship

When a bull has gathered a harem, other "satellite" bulls may try to steal a few cows for their own, so the herd bull is constantly on the lookout for other bulls or cows straying too far away.

This competition ensures only the strongest males mate, so the herd can remain healthy.

Bull elk in their prime, ages 5 to 10, are typically the ones with harems. A bull will mate with the cows in his harem over the course of two to three months, between August and October. Young bulls can mate, but usually don't if an older male is around. Cow elk 2 years and older can have calves, but cows 3 to 10 have the best chance of producing a calf. After the rut, bulls go off alone to feed and rest, and to heal from battle wounds. Then cow elk regroup as they make their way to winter range, following ancient paths memorized by the lead cows.

Warm & Cozy
Pregnancy

A cow elk carries her growing baby inside her through the winter and early spring for about eight months—about three weeks less than a human mother carries her baby.

The new elk calf has as much chance of being a boy as it does of being a girl. Unlike deer, elk rarely have twins.

Inside its mother, the calf is small at first. As it grows it needs more nutrition so it will be strong when it is born. In spring, grass grows green and tall, and new shoots sprout from the tips of shrubs and trees, providing nutritious food the mother needs to stay vigorous and have a healthy baby.

The larger and stronger a calf is at birth, the greater chance it will survive into adulthood.

TINE TIPS

In healthy habitat about 80 percent, or 8 out of every 10 cows, have calves each year.

Delivery Day
Birth

Most elk calves are born in late
May or June—perfect timing!

In May and June, the days have started to warm after the long winter. Being born in spring also gives the calf plenty of time to grow larger before winter sets in again. A cow usually gives birth in a special place between its wintering grounds and where it spends the summer. Calving grounds have plenty of food and water for the mother and hiding places for the baby under brush or trees.

A healthy elk calf weighs about 35 pounds at birth. That may seem like one big baby, but considering it weighs up to 1,000 pounds full-grown, a newborn calf is really quite small. When a calf is ready to be born, its mother moves away from other elk for a few days. Cow elk give birth standing up. The calf is often born front feet first, then its head, and then the rest of its body. Within moments of birth, the cow elk licks her calf dry.

Then the mother encourages her tiny calf to stand. Slowly the newborn finds its feet and stands on wobbly legs. As soon as it stands, it must move from the place it was born so it has a clean, dry place to sleep. After moving a few steps away from the birthing place, the new calf turns to nurse at its mother's side.

Safe & Sound

The First
Days of Life

For the first six weeks of its life, milk provides all the nutrients the calf needs.

A calf nurses four to six times a day, which doesn't seem like very often. But when it nurses—*it nurses!*—drinking more than 4 cups (32 ounces) of milk at each feeding. That's one big baby bottle! It adds up to over a gallon of milk a day!

After nursing, the calf curls up and sleeps, while its mother moves away to feed. If mom stayed close by, she might give away the calf's hiding place. A calf is too small to run from danger, so it will be safer by itself. The calf has almost no scent, and its spotted coat helps it blend into its surroundings. For up to four days, its mother will return for only a few minutes a day to nurse. But don't worry. She never forgets where she left her baby. If the calf needs her, it "bleats" like a lamb to call to her, and she reassures it with a soft "whine." If the cow barks an alarm call to warn danger is near, her calf will lower its head and stay as still as a rock until the danger passes. If she has to, mom will defend her calf by turning on a smaller predator such as a coyote and striking it with her front hooves. She will try to lead larger predators away by getting them to chase her.

WILDVISIONS.NET

45

Calf Kindergarten

The Nursery Herd

Do elk calves have a babysitter?

During its first 5 months of life, a calf will gain an average of two pounds a day. So just four days after its birth, it is already nearly 50 pounds and is sleeping less and moving around more. It is time to join the nursery herd of other cows with calves. With lots of grown-up eyes and ears looking and listening for danger, the calves are safer in a group while they sleep and frolic together. In the nursery herd, one of the cows looks after the calves as the other mothers venture off to feed. Each calf still knows which cow is its mother, and only its mother feeds it, but it spends most of the day with the other calves. The cows take turns babysitting, so all have a chance to eat.

The nursery herd stays together for about six weeks. During this time the mother has to move around often to find enough nutritious food to eat to feed herself and make milk for her baby. Left with a babysitter, the calf doesn't have to move as often, which lets it rest and grow strong. In addition, in the event of sudden danger, calves focus on the babysitter, and run with her. When the danger passes, each calf will call out for its mother. Eventually each cow locates her own calf. After nursing and being reassured that all is well, the calf will go back to the babysitter.

The Real World
Busting into the Herd

After six weeks, the elk calf has doubled its weight and is a whopping 110 pounds.

Once calves are 6 to 8 weeks old, they have grown so big that they are strong enough to run with the main herd, which has been slowly grazing their way toward summer range.

At 8 weeks, an elk calf begins to feed on vegetation. The cow elk will not completely stop nursing its calf until about seven months later in early winter, around the same time that the calf loses its spotted coat and grows its first warm winter coat. When a calf is weaned, it may weigh 300 pounds! By the end of its second summer, it will weigh almost as much as a full-grown adult. A female calf may live with or near its mother for the rest of its life. Male calves stay with the herd until the second autumn of life, when older bulls chase them away during mating season. Then the young bulls remain alone or hang out with a group of other young bulls.

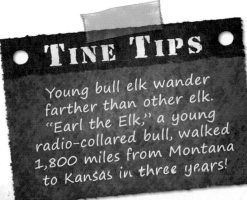

TINE TIPS

Young bull elk wander farther than other elk. "Earl the Elk," a young radio-collared bull, walked 1,800 miles from Montana to Kansas in three years!

Being out on its own for the first time is stressful for a young bull. Without the protection of the herd, many young bulls die from predators and many other causes. The percentage varies, but due to these deaths, the number of adult bulls compared to cows (bull to cow ratio) usually falls to about 25 bulls for every 100 cows.

The Big Move
Migration

Between October and December, most elk migrate, moving down from snowcapped mountains into low hills and valleys.

At times during migration, elk move quickly, traveling 20 to 30 miles a day. They often follow ancient paths used by their ancestors over hundreds or even thousands of years.

ACTIVITY
Play a game of Follow-the-Leader. Let each friend or student have a turn to be the leader. Explain that the leader must think about the easiest path to help the other elk and calves arrive safely at their winter range. This means they must walk, find an easy way around obstacles, avoid predators and find safe places to let the others rest. What makes a good leader?

Elk follow different migration routes depending on where they live. Elk that summer in the mountains move lower to foothills or valleys for the winter. Elk that live on a prairie may move down-river. A perfect winter range has a southern exposure to the sun or is on ridges where the wind blows away the snow. Elk may migrate only a few miles or more than 100 miles. Where it is warm year round, elk might simply move from the northern side of a hill where it is cooler in summer to the southern side of a hill where it is warmer in winter.

Elk stay as long as they can in their summer range. They move when the snow gets too deep or food becomes scarce. Most elk and their calves can handle snow that is a foot-and-a-half deep. When the snow gets deeper, the lead cow breaks a path through it that the herd can follow. This helps the pregnant cows survive winter by expending as little energy as possible.

PAUL QUENEAU

In spring, elk slowly move back up to their summer range. This usually occurs between April and June, with the herd moving about 1½ miles a day. By July they may be at the tops of the highest mountains. Then the herd spreads out in smaller groups to feed. Sometimes a herd will intermingle with herds from other areas. However, in autumn, each herd will return to its own winter range where hundreds or even thousands of elk gather.

Some cow elk live to be 20 years old, and some bulls to 15. Elk that migrate will repeat their trek every year of their life.

Elk in Peril
Death and Survival

Like most wild animals, elk face danger on a daily basis.

LEAGUE of PREDATORS

WOLF

GRIZZLY BEAR

BLACK BEAR

MOUNTAIN LION

Elk die in many ways. A predator might capture and eat an elk. If a drought or harsh winter lasts too long, an elk might die of starvation. A bull might get fatally injured while fighting another bull. In the wild, an elk might break its leg or suffer a puncture wound from a stick or branch while running. Insects such as ticks, mites and flies can weaken an elk. Some elk can get sick and die. However, these events usually happen to one or just a few elk at a time, and healthy elk can withstand most difficulties.

TINE TIPS

Elk rarely confront and attack a large predator. They usually run away. However, an individual cow may defend its calf, striking out with its hooves.

People cause other problems for elk.

A car might hit an elk that crosses a road. Near ranches, elk might get caught in fences. However, the biggest threat to elk is the loss of habitat. As early as 1785, people noticed that elk populations were declining. Since then, human development such as cities and highways have pushed elk into ever-smaller areas of land. In the late 1800s, along with hunting elk for food, settlers killed elk for their hides, antlers or for their ivory teeth. Two elk populations in the United States, the Merriam's elk and the Eastern elk, became extinct, and the remaining elk neared extinction. By 1907, only about 100,000 elk roamed North America.

PAUL QUENEAU

Working Together
How People Can Help Elk

Today, many people help elk. Conservation organizations, private landowners and public land managers work together to provide large tracts of land where elk can live.

They also work hard to improve habitat through careful use of activities such as fire, forest thinning and weed spraying. These are all efforts to provide elk with places to live year-round.

Radio Collar

Researchers are always trying to learn more about elk. They may capture an elk to weigh and measure it or to put on a radio collar. Radio collars allow biologists to know where the elk go and how they use their habitat. Teachers help, too, by educating students about wildlife, including elk.

Hunting plays an essential role in conserving elk. It builds a broad base of public support for wildlife, and it helps land managers and wildlife biologists manage elk populations. Hunting is not allowed in spring when elk are calving or in summer when they are taking care of their calves. Though some hunting occurs in winter, most hunting is in fall. Local hunting regulations change from year to year as needed to control the size of the herd and keep it healthy.

Children's high-pitched voices are a perfect match for calling in elk. Try to mimic elk chirps, mews and bugles using a simple plastic or cardboard tube.

With so much habitat now covered with cities and farms, we will probably never again see 10 million elk roaming North America.

Thanks to the dedication of conservation-minded people, elk numbers have rebounded over the last 100 years.

Today, over 1 million elk once again roam free and wild across North America.

Index

About the Author

Donna Love

Artist and award-winning author Donna Love has written numerous nature books for young people. She regularly brings her interactive natural history and art programs to grade schools and public events in Montana and the Pacific Northwest. Her motto, "The more you know about something, the better care you can give it," is why she likes to help people learn more about an animal or place.

Donna makes her home in Seeley Lake, Montana. She lives only minutes away from the Blackfoot-Clearwater Game Range, where in winter she sees elk on a weekly basis roaming the hills near her home.

Her husband Tim is a district ranger for the U.S. Forest Service. They have three grown children and one granddaughter. To see Donna's other work, go to her website, *www.donnalove.com*.

About the Artist

Christina Wald

Christina Wald has done illustration and design for a wide variety of toys, games, books and magazines. She graduated from the University of Cincinnati with a degree in Industrial (product) Design.

In addition to illustrating *Henry the Impatient Heron* (Mom's Choice Award Gold Medal Winner), which was written by Donna Love, Christina has illustrated other children's books, including *Habitat Spy, Little Red Bat, Black Beauty, Big Cats, Do Dolphins Really Smile* and many others ...

She lives in Cincinnati, Ohio, with her husband. Learn more at her website, *www.christinawald.com*.

Art Direction & Layout: Paul Marshall Allen
Edited by: Paul Queneau & Jan Brocci

FIELD NOTES
Elk & Other
Wildlife Sightings

Date:_____ Species: _____ Location: _____

Description: _____

Date:_____ Species: _____ Location: _____

Description: _____

Date:_____ Species: _____ Location: _____

Description: _____

Date:_____ Species: _____ Location: _____

Description: _____

Date:_____ Species: _____ Location: _____

Description: _____

Date:_____ Species: _____ Location: _____

Description: _____

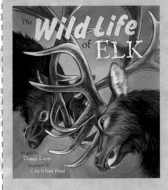

THIS BOOK
BELONGS TO

_____

THIS BOOK
BELONGS TO

_____

THIS BOOK
BELONGS TO

_____